The Data Governance Guidebook and Playbook

By a Practitioner for Practitioners

Kimberly K. Wienzierl

Technics Publications

115 Linda Vista

Sedona, AZ 86336 USA

https://www.TechnicsPub.com

Edited by Jamie Hoberman

Cover design by Lorena Molinari

First Printing 2021

Copyright © 2021 by Kimberly K. Wienzierl

ISBN, print ed.   9781634629621
ISBN, Kindle ed. 9781634629638
ISBN, ePub ed.   9781634629645
ISBN, PDF ed.   9781634629652

Library of Congress Control Number: 2021943378

Acknowledgments

I hope you find this book to be a good reference guide on your data governance journey. It was built out of many requests over the last decade for more information about how this framework worked at two companies and one government entity. Much of the content was learned from data greats like David Loshin, William McKnight, David Marco, and Robert Seiner. Many thanks to those who contributed over the years, including Mike Brady, Marc Daniels, David Kenney, Cheryl Verbeke, Heather Strode, Amber O'Connell, and Robyn Mace. Thanks to Kari Winger for contributing artwork and JP McInnes and Josh Edwards for continued support. A gigantic thank you to the hundreds of people that have executed this framework with me.

Contents

Introduction

Data management is a series of actions taken by the enterprise to maximize the accessibility and usability of data and to treat data as an asset. Data management provides a consistent, repeatable, and reliable approach to data planning, data solution design, data quality, and data controls. The foundational goal of data management is to maximize the business value of information across the enterprise.

The specific goals for data management are:

- Data assets are defined and organized to help meet business objectives.

- Users trust that the data is fit for use and available when needed.

- Users can securely access data with ease and clarity regarding content.

- Data can be integrated to the degree necessary to support business objectives.

- Data solutions can be delivered effectively, efficiently, and at the speed of business.

- The organization can adapt quickly to changing technology and business requirements.

- Continuous reduction in the total cost of data management and storage.

Data management addresses the following stages in the life cycle of information:

1. Data strategy
2. Data governance
3. Data movement (sourcing and staging)
4. Data storage
5. Data security
6. Data control and retention
7. Data access and usage

A standard approach to enterprise data will enable processes, applications, and platforms to reliably deliver accurate, complete, timely, consistent, accessible, and ultimately trusted information.

This book addresses data governance and its relationship to core data management. It will guide you on translating this commitment of managing data as an asset into a daily practice through the creation and ongoing usage of a data governance framework or program at your company or institution.

This book will advance the understanding and quality of data at your company or institution. It is your guide to implementing and performing data governance on any scale. It is a culmination of decades of experience and trial and error implementations of data governance. There are many different ways to "do" data governance, so this is a consolidated framework that has been researched, developed, honed, piloted, and implemented at many different-sized organizations across many industries. This book is your jump-start or shortcut to get you quickly into "doing" data governance versus trying to learn how to do it through your own research and study. It is a flexible framework that gives you a bit more than the basics and does not lock you into a model that does not fit. Mold it to fit your needs.

This book is a reference guide for employees, contractors, temporary employees, consultants, and authorized agents of your company or function who govern, manage, or develop data, including:

- Data owners
- Data stewards
- Data custodians
- Data analysts
- Application developers
- Database administrators
- Data producers
- Data consumers

This book is a resource to go to when you need to answer questions about data governance. It will help you manage the creation, transformation, and usage of data owned by or in the care of your enterprise. This book will not cover every data-related topic of interest, but it will guide you on the foundational topics for data governance.

Good luck on your data governance journey! Reach out to kim@wienzierl.com if you have questions or datagov.godaddysites.com for templates.

CHAPTER 1

About Data Governance

Data governance and data management are two distinct but tightly integrated components of the overall managing and governing of data. The definitions of these components are based on the work of John Ladley (Ladley, 2012).

Data governance ("The Principle")

Data governance is ensuring that data is managed properly and in accordance with defined standards. It addresses the conceptual data assets and provides guidance on data roles, definitions, rules, and controls. Good data governance provides both the data management framework and assurance that the framework is operating as designed.

Data management ("The Practice")

Data management is the day-to-day handling of data as it is created, transformed, transported, and consumed by business users. It addresses physical data assets.

DAMA International (https://www.dama.org/) has published the Data Management Body of Knowledge (DMBOK) which is a model for data management where Data governance resides in the center of the wheel:

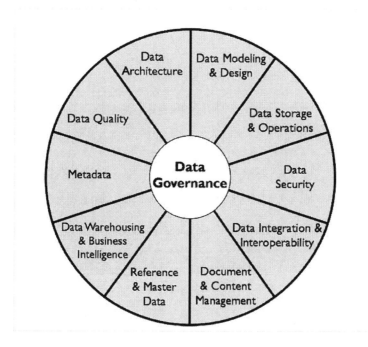

Figure 1. The DAMA DMBOK Wheel (Data Management Body of Knowledge, 2nd Edition, DAMA International, Technics Publications, 2017, page 36)

This book will focus on data governance, but you may notice frequent reference to data management processes or deliverables resulting from data governance activities.

The guiding principles behind this data governance framework are as follows:

Data Governance Principles (adopted from works of David Loshin and Robert Seiner):

Principle #1: Data is recognized as a valued and strategic enterprise asset.

Principle #2: Accountability for data is clearly defined, recorded, and enforced.

Principle #3: Data is managed to follow internal and external best practices, rules and regulations.

Principle #4: Data quality is defined and managed consistently across the data lifecycle.

These four data governance principles must be withheld throughout the lifecycle of the data that is being governed. They will help to keep the focus on the benefits of managing quality data for better and faster decision-making.

Types of data

At the highest level, enterprise data assets fit into three major types:

- Unstructured data (emails, social media, audio files, video, etc.)

- Semi-structured data (telematics, clickstream website usage metrics)

- Structured data (organized data in application databases and data stores)

Data governance concerns all types of data because it can provide business value if properly used and pose a significant business risk if misused. Typically, the unstructured and semi-structured data approach focuses on securing the data and finding analytical methods for extracting valuable information. The approach to governing structured data has these goals as well. Still, it includes more rigor around data definition and stewardship because of the complex integrations between business applications that create, consume, and transform this data.

Structured data includes the types shown in the pyramid below:

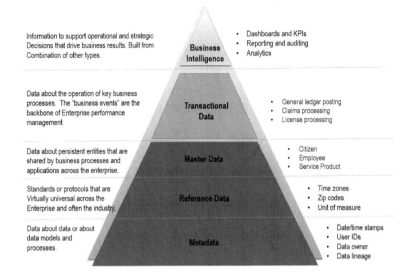

Figure 2. The Data Types Pyramid

Data governance aims to establish processes for managing all types of data deemed key or critical as data is created, moved, transformed, stored, and aggregated so that the business value of data is preserved and the data is readily available in a usable form.

CHAPTER 2

About Data Quality

Planning, strategy and business context are essential to effective data quality improvement.

Everyone is responsible for the quality of data, not just IT. Collaboration yields the best data quality results.

Focus on the *most critical data first*. Ignore data where acceptable data quality cannot be guaranteed.

Consider *data that is of the greatest benefit* to the majority of users and to the most diverse uses.

Work on benefit areas where data can be cleaned at the *best effort-cost relationship*.

Promote self-governed data quality, with a balance between issue prevention and remedy after the fact.

Automate data manipulation processes to avoid human errors.

Figure 3. Guiding principles for improving data quality

These principles may seem simple at first read, but after applying deep thought to each one, you will discover that they are especially useful to decide where to start, prioritize what happens next, train and communicate across the organization, and in choosing what mantras you will adopt on your journey to improving data quality.

Let's walk through each one a little deeper…

Planning, strategy, and business context

Planning, strategy, and business context are essential to effect data quality improvement.

Simply stated, data quality improvements rarely happen on accident or coincidentally. A concerted effort must be taken with defined roles to improve data quality. This does not mean that you have to hire a small army of people to do this. Usually, these people are already on staff and hold the skills and knowledge to work through any given data quality improvement and should become part of their everyday job if it is not already.

Everyone is responsible for data quality, not just IT. Collaboration yields the best data quality results.

I have an analogy I use to explain when IT became the "owner" of data. True or not, it usually gets the point across. Before computers, the accounting department owned a set of physical books they called their ledgers. They were responsible for them. They kept them accurate. They locked them in the safe at night. They noted who made adjustments to them when changes were documented. Then along came the computer. This physical book became an electronic file that the accounting department could not physically protect anymore. So this physical protection moved to IT. But at the same time, some "ownership" also moved with "ownership" being defined as protection, accuracy, timeliness, tracking, adjustments, etc. The responsibility moved too far, and now we have spent decades trying to move some of the responsibility back to the business that knows their data best.

Focus on the most critical data first. Ignore data where acceptable data quality cannot be guaranteed.

Well, ignore is a pretty strong word, but with so much to work on, maybe work on the critical data where you can have the most success first then second then third, etc. Reasons where data quality cannot be guaranteed might be if the data arrives from the outside and you cannot control the data quality processes like data from the federal government. Another reason might be because the data originates in an antiquated system where it is not feasible or realistic to put edits in upfront to improve data quality.

Consider data that can be of the greatest benefit to the majority of users and the most diverse uses.

This refers to working on the data improvement areas where there is the biggest bang for the buck but at the same time, work in small manageable pieces. The broader the impacted base, the more opportunity you have for that "big win" and to capture the attention of others who want the same. It is easiest to stay within a given department because working with departments adds new wrinkles for communication, prioritization, and funding.

Work on benefit areas where data can be cleaned at the best effort-cost benefit.

It may not be cost-effective to improve current data quality and then go back and fix 30 years of archived data. At some point, a line needs to be drawn in the sand where it makes sense that the benefit does not outweigh the cost to improve data quality.

Promote self-governed data quality, with a balance between issue prevention and remedy after the fact.

Once the data owner is in place, they should manage the control plan that measures the quality of their data. They should own the remediation steps to get the data quality under control if it happens to slip. They are the ones that develop and hold the plan for continuous improvement of their data, including stopping bad data from being created or ingested and, worst case, correcting data on the go.

Automate data manipulation processes to avoid human error.

You may be familiar with the term "dummy proof." It means to not allow humans to intervene in the processing of production data in a manner that can degrade data quality. This can be accomplished in several ways like pick lists, reference data checks, and general data security controls.

Guiding principles for data management

This list of guiding principles is fairly lengthy, so you may choose to start with a smaller list then consciously add more to the list each year as you mature and prove that you can work under your adopted guiding principles.

Recognize and manage data as a strategic and valuable enterprise asset.

---

1. Departments shall keep an up-to-date inventory of all data elements

2. Data owners must exist for all critical or key data

3. Source of record will be clearly defined

4. Data is managed consistently across its data lifecycle

Publish training, policies, and standards to formalize data processes.

---

1. Data governance policies shall address data architecture, data quality, metadata management, master data management (MDM), data security, data privacy, database recovery, data retention, data access, data sharing, document and content management, and other industry best practices and standards.

2. Data governance policies shall clearly outline and define the roles and responsibilities of data owners, data stewards, and data custodians.

3. Data standards shall address data warehousing, business intelligence, analytics, metadata management, master data management, data

modeling, and data architecture, including naming conventions, data dictionaries, definitions standards, and standard abbreviations.

4. There should be a formal MDM structure, which includes a taxonomy, glossary of terms, definition, and keywords, and assigns consistent responsibilities.

5. A metadata creation and maintenance policy shall be comprised of mandatory standards to ensure data integrity.

6. A data security policy shall address ways to manage data security, data encryption standards and mechanisms, access guidelines, transmission protocols, documentation requirements, remote access standards, breach incident reporting procedures, access to data using mobile devices, and data storage on portable devices with records management policies.

7. A data privacy policy shall be followed that addresses all applicable data regulations, such as HIPAA, FERPA, FIPS, CJIS, PCI, FTI, and PII.

8. There shall be a written plan outlining the processes for monitoring compliance with the established data governance, security, and privacy policies and standards.

9. There shall be a checklist or standard template for data set data governance documentation.

10. Data governance training will cover roles, responsibilities, data quality accountability, data usability, integrity, availability and security, general data fluency, data tools, and data reporting guidance.

Ensure data quality at the source.

---

1. Correct data at the source.

2. Eliminate free text fields where possible, utilizing drop-down menus and reference tables.

3. Limit the number of people who can create or modify data.

4. Do not let "bad" data enter the data store.

5. No ongoing programmatic data cleansing (validate and cleanse upon creation/ingestion)

6. Information Technology (IT) will own no data or data corrections.

7. It will be the exception, not the rule, to extend the out-of-the-box data models.

8. Business process management may be needed for data quality management.

9. Ensure data quality matches planned usage.

10. There shall be well-defined, documented data change and quality control processes.

11. Each department shall have a data quality management plan that:

   a) Plans for the assessment of the current state and identification of key metrics for measuring data quality.

   b) Identifies the data issues that are critical to achieving business objectives.

   c) Identifies key data quality dimensions.

   d) Defines the business rules critical to ensuring high-quality data.

   e) Deploys processes for measuring and improving the quality of data.

   f) Acts to resolve any identified issues to improve data quality.

   g) Promotes data quality awareness that includes referencing data issues and the associated business and technical impacts.

Achieve easily accessible data and information.

---

1. Data is shared.

    a) Under no circumstances will the data sharing principle cause confidential data to be compromised.

    b) Data made available for sharing will be relied upon by users to execute their respective tasks.

2. Requirements shall be collected, and related processes documented, reviewed, and verified when data reporting and analysis are considered in the Software Development Life Cycle

3. There shall be data recovery, backup, and retention plans for all databases and servers.

4. All critical or key data has a clearly documented and communicated definition that is understandable and available to all users.

5. A data framework/methodology will be applied to all critical or key data.

6. Eliminate point-to-point integration between applications and utilize a data hub for sharing non-transactional data.

Ensure data information security and privacy.

---

1. Department data inventories will apply a data confidentiality classification analysis based on the level of risk with adherence to policies and standards.

2. Mechanisms to mask or hide confidential data shall be used when appropriate.

3. There shall be a clearly documented and published process for managing data access, views, and permissions, including on-boarding and off-boarding employees.

Prioritize and incorporate these guiding principles over time. It is also a good place to assess the success of your data governance program by measuring the maturity against those adopted principles.

CHAPTER 3

Guidebook and Playbook Overview

This book is both a data governance guidebook and playbook. It "guides" or offers instruction for what to do to accomplish and sustain data governance and also asks questions to trigger the work to be done in each element of the data governance framework

The Data Governance Guidebook aims to describe the key aspects of the eight elements of data governance. Learn the goals, potential inputs and outputs, and templates or tools you may use to complete the data governance tasks.

The purpose of the Data Governance Playbook is to ask you trigger questions to aid in completing the work needed for each of the eight elements of data governance. If you do not know where to start, start here. At the end of each section describing each element, there will be a list of several questions you may ask yourself and work to answer to complete the work necessary for that element. This is the Data Governance Playbook.

Additionally, you will find in Chapter 4, a blank template to document your evidence or artifacts as you move data under this data governance framework. Consider this like an electronic "3 ring binder" of everything related to data governance for a well-defined and well-scoped set of data. The data owner is typically the owner of this data governance document and will be the person to self-audit the process. External auditors may also use the data governance document (completed playbook) to accelerate their auditing of your data governance processes, data controls, or data quality practices. This is helpful because it is all documented in one place with links to documentation or evidence showing that the data governance processes are being carried out as planned.

Who else will use the completed Data Governance Playbook? It may be used by the data management team, data owners, data stewards, internal and external auditors, and anyone else interested in the specifics of a certain data category or domain. By referencing the completed playbook, a person can learn about who owns the data, how it is defined and how it flows, the governing policies, procedures, standards, and security controls related to the data, and what metrics manage the data audit cycle.

The recipe for a successful data governance program follows. Like any other recipe, you can and should make this your own. Start with small batches, then "bake" for a crowd. Try out your recipe on "friends and family" first or, in this case, your closest and most forgiving internal customers. Eventually, you will start modifying the recipe to suit your tastes and needs and apply it consistently yet tailor it to the audience. This is just one recipe. As you can imagine, there are thousands of more recipes for data governance. Use the best parts as you build out and apply your data governance strategy.

Overview of the eight elements

The data governance process contains eight elements or phases, each with its own goals and deliverables.

Figure 4. The eight elements of data governance

This diagram shows the eight elements of data governance. While it is not necessary to have each element in a completely mature state before starting the next, the sequence has an inherent and intuitive logic. You start with "managing" the data, then move into "controlling" the data, and then on to "sustaining" the data quality level.

This is a flexible framework for doing data governance. As mentioned before, there is a bit of an inherent order of events across the eight elements. Element #1 is

Organization. This is where you decide the scope of the data to be governed and business ownership of the data. It should be done first. The rest have some dependencies you will uncover as you work through the elements, such as data procedures for data policies, but most can be worked concurrently to some degree.

The methodology

A data governance program will build a methodology around the eight elements of data governance. This, combined with the playbook's reference templates, processes, responsibility charts, task examples, and sample deliverables, leads to a lightweight methodology that collects what is needed to be known about critical or key data to be managed as an asset. In many cases, similar data governance work is already underway at your organization, maybe in several places, in an uncontrolled and dissimilar fashion, so this methodology will pull it all together in a common fashion. It will be an ongoing effort to bring these together across all business areas with common objectives. This is not a do it once and it is done function. Data governance is an ongoing process shared between business and IT.

Now, let's dig into the eight elements of data governance.....

Eight Elements of the Data Governance Framework

Organization

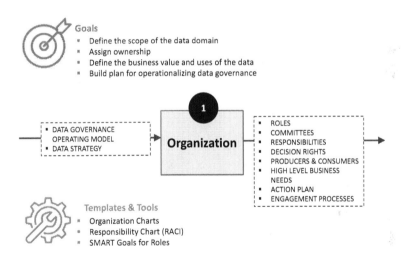

Figure 5. The Organization element of data governance

Effective data governance requires the coordinated work effort of skilled people who share common goals and have clearly defined roles, responsibilities, and decision rights.

This section will describe the data governance roles, which includes governing bodies, key role definitions, and an overview of organizational structures at the enterprise and data domain levels. Executive leadership supporting data governance or an established data governance committee carries out this element.

The goals of the **Organization** element are the same for every level of data governance from the enterprise level on down to individual data elements: define the scope of the data, assign an owner, define the business value, identify the needs of data stakeholders and create a plan for operationalizing data governance.

The inputs to consider when working on the Organization element could be an existing data strategy or data governance operating model. Reference them if you already have these to complete this element. If you do not, then proceed without any inputs or use your own inputs, such as organizational charts or team charters.

Deliverables for the Organization element include who is doing what with the data, the scope of the data to be put under governance, who has decision rights regarding the data, and scoping the high-level need of why the data should be governed.

Data governance roles

I based the following data governance role model on a data governance operating model originally described by Robert Seiner (Seiner, 2014). These roles are typically not full-time positions but rather a work goal for those employees with these titles. Therefore, chances are they are already doing similar work that will tie in nicely to the Data Governance Framework methodology.

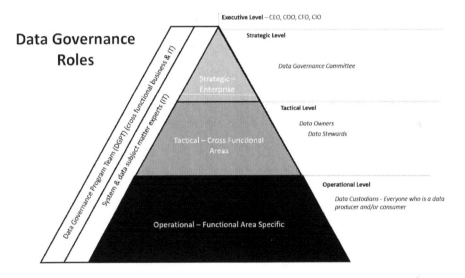

Figure 6. Data governance roles

Executive level sponsor

Responsibilities:

- Fill positions for a data governance committee or other data governing bodies.

- Support and assist in changing the company's culture to treat data as an asset.

- Focus attention to data improvements with a manageable scope.

- Advocate a culture of data-driven decision-making and support through evangelism and funding.

- Help to resource initiatives for data improvement.

Data governance committee

Responsibilities:

- Provide strategic direction for enterprise data governance.

- Champion the marketing and messaging regarding managing data as an asset.

- Endorse and enforce enterprise data governance:
    o Policies
    o Procedures
    o Strategy

- Resolve escalated conflicts between data stakeholders.

- Prioritize, approve, and resource data governance initiatives.

- Recommend strategic business investments regarding data.

- Meet regularly to oversee data governance program status.

The data governance committee is chartered under a documented team charter that describes the purpose, roles, membership, and committee cadence. Here is an example of a data governance committee team charter from the State of Tennessee.

#####

Purpose

The State views data governance as a fundamental component of doing business and is committed to stewarding data, protecting information assets, and guiding Departments on maintaining their information so that self-serve quality data is available for operations and analytics. The Strategic Technology Solutions (STS) CIO on behalf of the State has identified the need to build a cross domain, interdisciplinary committee inclusive of information technology and business to address data governance and standards in a holistic way. This charter establishes the STS Data Governance Committee, a multi-agency collaboration, whose purpose is to provide a stabilizing influence so a common understanding of the value of data as an asset is collaborated across all lines of services and to develop, maintain, and implement a common set of data guidelines and standards; to serve the State's data community. The Data Governance

Committee functions as a decision-making body representative of all participating stakeholders. The Data Governance Committee is responsible for both promoting a common vision across the State, and for ensuring compliance with Tennessee's data guidelines and practices.

Scope

This charter applies to the Tennessee State Government's Executive Branch and its organizational units that are directly responsible for developing, deploying, or consuming data services. It describes the roles and, responsibilities for, policies, and procedures that govern the operation of the Data Governance Committee. A primary member and a delegate member from each of the agencies are invited and encouraged to attend and participate.

Responsibilities

The Data Governance Committee is responsible for contributing to the overarching guidance concerning the policy, practice, and implementation of data governance in support of the Departments, and the State's mission and vision.

Responsibilities for Data Governance Committee members include:

- Ensuring data strategy, standards, policies and procedures are in place and reviewed regularly so high-quality data that supports objectives is available;

- Ensure the State is well positioned to exploit advances in data and analytics;

- Charter work and find resources as needed to advance improvements and understanding of data;

- Approve, prioritize and adopt work related to improvements in data quality (such as data accuracy improvements, data definitions, data roles and ownership, data policies, data quality metrics, benefits of data improvements);

- Perform business risk management actions to ensure sustainability of the data improvement efforts;

- Resolve conflicts in data definitions, values, and usage;

- Drive consistency and leverage reuse in data initiatives across the State;

- Suggest and support training and workforce development as it relates to data;

- Provide oversight, governance and management for projects relating to data;

- Deliver enterprise communications regarding awareness and direction about data;

- Assist in the establishment of data quality and data maturity metrics;

- Establish and use a change control process for data policies, processes, and standards;

- Approval of data guidelines

- Appoint and charter Data Governance workgroups to assist with development of procedures, practice, and standards;

- Annually review this Data Governance Committee Charter and data policies, processes, and standards.

Organization

Sponsors

The Sponsors of the Data Governance Committee will act as champions for the effort and express their support through communications and application of resources and priority. They may be called upon when consensus cannot be met by the Data Governance Committee or as a form of escalation.

Members

The Committee Members of the Data Governance Committee represent the Departments, Divisions, Offices, and Programs across the State as well as key STS personnel. Additional members may be added with a vote by the Data Governance Committee. Committee Members will commit to a 1-year term if possible and will have the option to recommend a replacement and rotate off after a year.

The Data Governance Committee will include all organizations that collect, store, use, or exchange data to support an operational or mission requirement. Others may be invited to support the data governance efforts by providing their expertise in specific areas. These may include support staff, meeting facilitators, advisors, subject matter experts, and liaisons to other relevant industry or technology organizations.

Most Data Governance decisions are anticipated to be reached by consensus; however, if consensus is unable to be reached, Data Governance Committee members will cast a vote. Data Governance members serve as representatives of their respective Department, Division, Office, or Program; however, they are charged with ensuring that the best interests of the State overall are served by their decisions. If an organization is not represented by one of the members shown in Appendix A, they may contact any committee member to obtain sponsorship or representation on the Data Governance Committee.

Chairperson

The Chairperson will preside over meetings and act as lead spokesperson for the Data Governance Committee between meetings. The Chairperson is responsible for drafting each meeting's agenda and sharing it at least seven days prior to the start of a meeting. They are responsible for keeping order and being fair and impartial throughout the decision-making process.

Secretary

The Secretary will commit to documenting the meeting decisions and discourse and will be sharing each meeting's minutes at least seven days prior to the start of the next meeting. The Secretary will be responsible for maintaining an up-to-date list of all members, notifying members of their election/appointment to sub-committee offices and providing them with documentation of their roles and responsibilities, casting of votes, and meeting minutes. The Secretary will be responsible for receiving requests for new membership, sponsorship, or representation. In the event the Secretary is unable to be present for a meeting, they may designate someone to serve in this capacity for that meeting.

Advisors and Subject Matter Experts (SMEs)

The advisors and subject matter experts from across the Enterprise will be invited to participate in the regular meetings of the Data Governance Committee. It is critical that they participate, providing their expertise to the sub-committee so well-informed decisions can be made. These advisors and subject matter experts as well as others from across the State's departments will be invited to participate in the focus group as the needs arise to work outside the committee to research and make recommendations on topics.

Policies and Procedures

Meetings

Data Governance Committee meetings and decision-making shall be presided over by the chairperson or by another appointed representative of the Data Governance Committee.

Meetings of the Data Governance Committee shall be announced with adequate time for arrangements and preparation. Background material and a final agenda shall be circulated in advance. Agendas will specify when a vote is scheduled and supporting information will be circulated at least a week before a vote is to be taken, whether at a face-to-face meeting or by electronic means.

Data Governance Committee meetings are normally scheduled for at least an hour on a monthly basis. Due to the responsibility of developing standards, and the review and approval of requests for service development, the committee may meet more often initially to expedite its response.

An action item log shall be maintained and reviewed at each meeting. Key decisions and next steps of meetings shall be distributed to the Data Governance Committee members for comment and revised accordingly.

Standing Meeting Agenda

- Introductions/Agenda
- Minutes and action from the last meeting
- Data Management Current Backlog & Prioritization of Work
- Key concept/progress/successes/issues
- Next Steps

Decision-making

Consensus is a core value of the Data Governance Committee. To promote consensus, the Data Governance Committee process requires the Chairperson to ensure that the group considers all legitimate views, proposals, and objections, and endeavors to reconcile them. When unanimity is not possible, the Data Governance Committee strives to make decisions that are supported by the available evidence, and then to submit the issue to vote.

A two-thirds majority vote from all voting members is required for a final decision with regards to changes to amend Charter or Governance Plan regardless of the voting method; all other votes can be passed by a simple majority (51%) of the quorum which is 2/3 of the committee. The Data Governance Committee may reach a decision by face-to-face meetings, teleconference, electronic communication, or any combination of the above.

Member Selection

When one or more seats become open on the Data Governance Committee, the Chairperson will launch a call for candidates from the organizations that have vacant positions. The Chairperson shall be authorized to recognize membership.

Attendance

Every member must make a concerted effort to attend all meetings (face-to-face meetings and teleconferences). Missing three out of four consecutive meetings is grounds for a vote to remove membership from the Data Governance Committee. The Chairperson shall have power to declare the position of a Member to be vacant in the event such Member or proxy is absent from three (3) consecutive meetings.

Openness & Confidentiality

Data Governance Committee meetings are open to outside attendance. The Chairperson may, upon informing the members, exclude invited participants and liaisons from discussion as required by the personnel, legal, or financial nature of the matter.

Focus Groups

The Data Governance Committee may delegate some of its responsibilities to certain focus groups to assist with continuing long-term activities or detailed analysis and planning prior to a decision-making of the Data Governance Committee, such as development of policies, procedures, guidelines, standards, and recommendations to STS for funding.

Focus Group Members

The Chair of each focus group shall be appointed by the Data Governance Committee from among its membership. The Chair's appointment shall be for a six-month term and the individual can be reappointed for consecutive terms by the Data Governance Committee. Other participants in the workgroup should be selected from subject matter experts across the State Enterprise.

Responsibilities of Focus Groups

Focus groups will be required to:

- Invite all interested parties to join;

- Submit a list of deliverables and their target dates to the Data Governance Committee;

- Make regular progress reports to the Data Governance Committee (these may be informal);

- Ensure that decisions and recommendations are accompanied by explanation that will support that consensus within the Data Governance Committee.

It is recognized that some individuals will join a Focus Group in order to follow, rather than participate in, discussions. This is acceptable, although workgroup members are encouraged to share their expertise with the community through active participation.

#####

Data owner

A data owner has the highest level of accountability for the integrity of an enterprise data domain or collection of domains. The data owner is typically a director level or higher. The data owners either sit on the data governance committee or have delegates representing them on the committee. The data owner is responsible for developing and overseeing their domain's data policies, procedures, controls, and metrics. The incumbent for this role should reside in the functional organization that owns the data domain as defined by the data governance committee.

The data owner serves as the sponsor and champion for establishing data governance in their data domain(s).

Responsibilities:

- Define the data elements in their domain.

- Identify and engage business users to understand their needs.

- Identify and assign data stewards.

- Develop and operationalize "The Eight Elements of Data Governance."

- Ensure the data domain policy is aligned with the enterprise data policy and standards.

- Work with other data domain owners to understand integration points.

- Escalate cross-domain issues to the data governance committee.

Data steward

A data steward is accountable for maintaining the desired level of data quality within their data domain(s). In support of this duty, they implement and enforce the data policies, procedures, controls, and metrics defined by the data owner to whom they are aligned.

Responsibilities:

- Define, monitor, and manage data quality for their domain.

- Prioritize data quality issues and lead root cause analyses.

- Assist in developing and maintaining data policies, standards, and controls.

- Ensure adoption of and compliance with domain data standards.

Data custodian

The Data custodian is responsible for ensuring that the creation and maintenance of data within their respective data domain(s) adhere to all relevant policies and procedures.

Responsibilities:

- Actively work on improving data quality.

- Work with data owners and data stewards to create and maintain data quality metrics.

- Assist in root cause analysis on data quality issues.

- Authorize the creation and maintenance of master data within their domain.

- Classify data access levels and authorize access.

- Implement data governance policies in the system of record.

- Enter data in compliance with the data standards.

Data producer

A data producer is any person that can author data in a system of record. Data producers may include both company employees and third parties such as suppliers or clients.

Responsibilities:

- Create data in accordance with policies and standards.

- Ensure that data is accurate, complete, and timely.

- Comply with all relevant security and access controls.

Data consumer

A data consumer is any person that can view the company data, whether in source systems or derived information products such as reports and dashboards. Consumers may include both company employees and third parties such as suppliers.

Responsibilities:

- View and use data in accordance with policies and standards.

- Ensure that data is accurate, complete, and timely by reporting if that is not the case.

- Comply with all relevant security and access controls.

Other data roles

There are data roles outside of the data governance and data management community of practice that impact data availability, usability, and integrity. These roles include application developers, technical data stewards, database administrators, and data testers.

Responsibilities:

- Understand and align to the defined data models.

- Understand and align with the definitions in the enterprise metadata repository.

- Comply with any data owner defined procedures and controls in the design of application solutions to manage data.

- Comply with data owner defined definitions, standards, and security in the design of applications and business intelligence products such as reports and dashboards.

- Ensure that data testing criteria adequately represents the requirements as defined by the data owner.

Now that you have defined the roles, another deliverable may be a RACI chart or simply a responsibility chart. A **RACI chart** will be referred to several times in this book. A RACI chart, also called a RACI matrix, clarifies roles and responsibilities, ensuring a clear understanding of each person's role and that all bases are covered for anything needing someone to be Responsible, Accountable, Consulted, or Informed. Another form of **RACI** is **RASCI** where the S is for Supporting.

The following page contains an example of a RACI chart. For Organization, your RACI chart may cover data responsibilities for a data category, an entire department, a data set, or any well-defined scope of data under data governance.

Data Governance Framework RACI	Executive Sponsor (Who?)	Executive Data Governance Committee	Data Owner (Who?)	Data Stewards (Who?)	Data Custodians (Who?)			
Developing Data Governance Organization	R	A	I					
Developing/Documenting/Updating Data Governance Policy	A	I	R	C				
Developing/Documenting/Updating Data Governance Procedures	A	I	R	R	C			
Developing/Documenting/Updating Data Standards and Definitions	I		A	R	C			
Documenting the Architecture of the Data and Systems	I		A	R	R			
Developing/Documenting/Updating Data Security and Controls. Pulling access records.	I		A	A	R			
Developing/Updating/Reporting Data Metrics	I	I	A	R	C			
Developing and Performing Data Audits	A	A	R	C	C			

Figure 7. Example RACI

SMART goals

Another deliverable to consider is **SMART goals** for the people who are assigned a data role. Here are some example SMART goals that could be universal across your enterprise.

Data owner SMART goal example

Support data governance efforts, encourage data culture, and increase data literacy by ensuring X% of employees complete the data governance overview training by (date).

Action items:

- Identify and engage business users to understand their data needs.

- Identify and assign data stewards.

- Work with other domain owners to understand integration points.

- Escalate cross-domain issues to the data governance committee.

- Recognize and manage data as a strategic and valuable enterprise asset.

- Regularly audit the data governance process for data you own.

- Measure and improve data quality for domains or data set that you own.

Data steward SMART goal example

Recognize and manage data as a strategic and valuable enterprise asset by creating an inventory of all critical data elements, publishing data definitions, and tracing critical data fields from source to use by (date).

Action items:

- Escalate identified data issues to the data governance committee.

- Define, monitor, and manage data quality.

- Prioritize data quality issues and lead root cause analyses.

- Assist in developing and maintaining data policies, standards, and controls.

- Ensure adoption of and compliance with data standards.

Data custodian SMART goal example

Ensure data governance standards and policies are followed by documenting and adhering to procedures surrounding the creation and maintenance of data by (date).

Action items:

- Actively work on improving data quality.

- Work with data owners and data stewards to create and maintain data quality metrics.

- Assist in root cause analysis for data quality issues.

- Classify data access levels and authorize access.

- Implement data governance policies.

- Enter data in compliance with the data standards.

- Eliminate free text fields where possible, utilizing drop-down menus and reference tables.

- Limit the number of people who can create/modify.

- Create a clearly documented and published process for managing data access, views, and permissions including onboarding and off boarding of employees.

Another possible deliverable from #1 Organization is an organization chart about the data under governance. You may have solid line organization charts, dotted line/matrixed organization charts, or project organization charts that identify the data roles needed for the data being put under governance.

Organization playbook

The following are questions to trigger action for Organization. In answering these questions and documenting the results, you will be well on your way to completing Element #1.

a. What organization owns the data?

b. What is the data owner's name?

c. When was data ownership started under this framework (date)?

d. Storage location of the RACI chart?

e. Who are the internal producers of the data?

f. Who are the external producers of the data?

g. Who are the internal consumers of the data?

h. Who are the external consumers of the data?

i. Who is the data governance committee representative for this data?

j. Who are the data stewards for this data, and what is their function?

k. Who are the data custodians for this data, and what is their function?

l. What is the scope of the data that is going under data governance, and what is its business purpose?

Policies

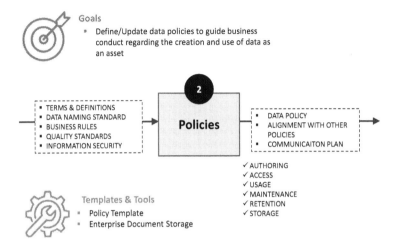

Figure 8. The POLICIES element of data governance

A **Policy** provides direction on appropriate business conduct and expected behavior consistent with your company's principles of good corporate governance. Policies are *principles* that guide the development of more specific instructions such as procedures and controls.

A Data Policy guides how we manage a data asset over the entire data lifecycle. There are five key focus areas for data policy development:

1. Authoring: When, how, and by whom data may be created, changed, or deleted. It is the regulation of the Create, Read, Update, Delete/Deactivate cycle.

2. Access: Which people or systems are authorized to get to the data?

3. Usage: What are the authorized uses for the data and how are they mapped to authorized users?

4. Maintenance: How is the data maintained in the source system(s) and backed up for recovery?

5. Retention/Storage: How long the data must be kept, in what format, and defined lead time for retrieval?

The level of policy definition required will vary depending upon the business value of the data and the associated risk identified by the data owner.

The goal of the Policy phase of data governance is to:

- Define new data policies.
- Update existing policies.

- Confirm alignment with enterprise policy and other domain-level policies.
- Communicate the commitment to a policy.

The data owner performs these activities with support from the data steward(s) and data governance committee, who can serve as a clearinghouse for best practices in data policy development and provide advice on interpreting existing data policies. The data owner must approve any new or updated policies.

If your company has existing enterprise policies and procedures related to data, please take note of them and reference them in your data governance playbook and any new data policies and procedures that get written where applicable. These may be corporate policies related to Software Development Life Cycle Management, Change Management, Information Security, Acceptable Use Policies, Third Party Access to User Accounts and Electronic Data—to name a few. Data owners and data stewards should begin here when developing new data policies to ensure alignment.

Other potential inputs to Policies could be terms and definitions that would be useful in drafting a data policy, data naming standards, business rules, predefined quality standards to achieve, and input from information security on data handling.

Another deliverable to consider with Policy is an organizational change management (OCM) plan. This plan will describe the people or groups of people who know about, understand, and abide by applicable data policies. The purpose of an OCM plan is to communicate the policies and reinforce that knowledge on some regular or triggered basis.

Some tools or templates to consider are a policy template if your enterprise already has policies. You will also want to seek out or establish a storage area for the policies that are easily accessible by those using the policies.

Policies playbook

The following are questions to trigger action for Policies. In answering these questions and documenting the results, you will be well on your way to completing Element #2.

a. Authoring: When, how, and by whom data may be created, changed, or deleted? It is the regulation of the Create, Read, Update, Delete/Deactivate (CRUD) cycle.

b. Access: Which people or systems are authorized to get to the data?

c. Usage: What are the authorized uses for the data and how are they mapped to authorized users?

d. Maintenance: How is the data maintained in the source system(s) and backed up for recovery?

e. Retention: How long must the data must be kept, in what format, and defined lead time for retrieval?

f. Storage: Where does this data physically reside, and how is it being protected?

g. Storage location of data policies for this data?

h. Is this data policy impacted by any other enterprise policy? If so, which one(s)?

i. When was the data policy communicated and to who and how?

Procedures

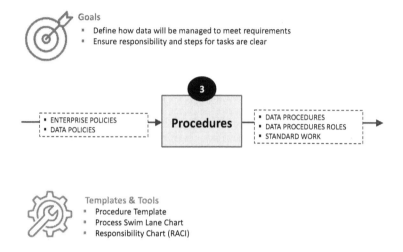

Figure 9. The Procedures element of data governance

A **Procedure** is a documented directive that specifies the way we work to ensure we meet the business objectives of our data policies. It defines what should be done, how it should be done, who should do it, under what circumstances, and with what decision rights.

In the Procedures element of data governance, the data owner and data steward determine what data governance procedures will be required to ensure that the data complies with data policies and meets business requirements. The goals of this phase include:

- Define how data will be managed to meet requirements day-to-day.

- Ensure responsibility for tasks are clear.

Inputs to consider are any enterprise-wide policies (and their related procedures) that apply to the data you are putting under governance, such as information security policies and the data policies you found or created in #2 Policies.

Key activities include:

- Identify which business processes create and consume the data.

- Document how data should be authored.

- Document how access to data will be provisioned and maintained.

- Define approval workflows.

Outputs from this element are drafted data procedures that include roles and steps to be taken by who and when.

Some tools or templates that could be used here might be a procedure template if your enterprise has a standard format, a RACI chart to describe the roles and responsibilities for executing the procedures, and a process swim lane chart that shows in a graphical form who is completing tasks in what order and at what time.

Procedures playbook

The following are questions to trigger action for Procedures. In answering these questions and documenting the results, you will be well on your way to completing Element #3.

a. Identify which business processes create and consume the data.

b. Document how data should be authored.

c. Document how access to data will be provisioned and maintained.

d. Define approval workflows.

e. Determine the RACI for who will be managing what data on a day-to-day basis.

f. Create the communication and training plan for this data regarding who will be doing what and when and how.

g. Document data procedures that already exist and what needs to be created.

h. Determine where the data procedures are stored.

i. Determine when the data procedure(s) was communicated and to who and how.

Standards and definitions

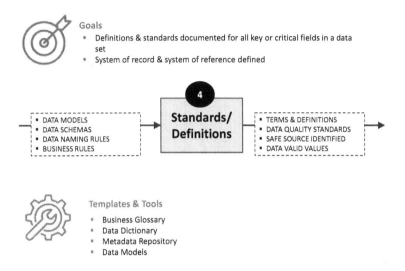

Goals
* Definitions & standards documented for all key or critical fields in a data set
* System of record & system of reference defined

| DATA MODELS
DATA SCHEMAS
DATA NAMING RULES
BUSINESS RULES | **4**
Standards/
Definitions | TERMS & DEFINITIONS
DATA QUALITY STANDARDS
SAFE SOURCE IDENTIFIED
DATA VALID VALUES |

Templates & Tools
* Business Glossary
* Data Dictionary
* Metadata Repository
* Data Models

Figure 10. The Standards and Definitions elements of data governance

Standards and definitions are the guidelines that inform how we design data solutions, interpret information, evaluate conformance and ensure quality for our data from source to consumer. The goals of this phase of data governance are:

- Definitions and standards documented for all required fields in the dataset.

- Safe source of data identified.

The data steward typically performs this work with support from the data management team. After the definitions and safe sources have been documented for the required data elements in the domain, the data owner reviews and approves them.

Definitions

Definitions describe the meaning of data elements in a language that data consumers easily understand. Each element of a data model that has meaning should have a documented definition. Providing this definition is the responsibility of the data owner.

Standards

Standards are the documented specifications for a specific data element or sub-element. Standards may include:

- Valid range of values for a data field.

- Specific formatting rules.

- Minimum data quality levels.

- Designation of mandatory or "golden" data fields.

- Identification of safe sources for data.

- Formulas for creating derived data within a data set.

This list is not exhaustive. Each data domain will have specific needs for standards, depending on the business value and enterprise risk associated with the domain. Inputs to consider with this data governance element could be existing data models or schemas, data naming rules, naming conventions, and applicable business rules.

Data dictionaries and business glossaries

A data dictionary and business glossary is a one-stop source for information about data within a dataset. It includes both terms and definitions as well as any data standards. It can contain other metadata such as the names of data owners, stewards, and custodians, the confidentiality level of the data, any "tags" to help index the data for searching, and comments from data producers and consumers about the data. This is also the place to document valid data values, types, formats, or ranges. If there are data quality standards or even data quality certifications about the data quality level, it could be noted in the data dictionary. This is also the place and time to note whether the data comes from a safe source.

Data dictionaries can be documents, spreadsheets, or reside in specialized software tools, such as the Alation Data Catalog, designed to ease the task of maintaining and using the dictionary as an enterprise guideline. These software tools can house the business glossary, data dictionary, and other metadata, and automate gathering some of the technical metadata. Data dictionaries may also exist for the physical data tables in a specific database management system (DBMS). These "local" data dictionaries must align with any enterprise metadata repository.

Standards/definitions playbook

The following are questions to trigger action for the Standards/definitions. In answering these questions and documenting the results, you will be well on your way to completing Element #4.

a. What are the key or critical data elements?

b. What are the valid values?

c. What is the technical information regarding the data element?

d. What are the data definitions?

e. What is the data model?

f. What is the storage location of data definitions and valid format for this data?

g. What is the storage location for valid value charts for this data?

Architecture

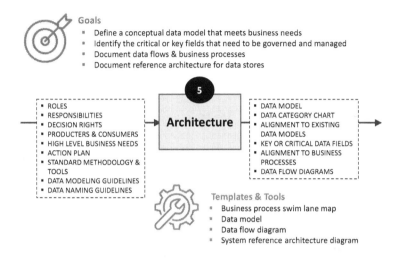

Goals
- Define a conceptual data model that meets business needs
- Identify the critical or key fields that need to be governed and managed
- Document data flows & business processes
- Document reference architecture for data stores

5

- ROLES
- RESPONSIBILITIES
- DECISION RIGHTS
- PRODUCERS & CONSUMERS
- HIGH LEVEL BUSINESS NEEDS
- ACTION PLAN
- STANDARD METHODOLOGY & TOOLS
- DATA MODELING GUIDELINES
- DATA NAMING GUIDELINES

Architecture

- DATA MODEL
- DATA CATEGORY CHART
- ALIGNMENT TO EXISTING DATA MODELS
- KEY OR CRITICAL DATA FIELDS
- ALIGNMENT TO BUSINESS PROCESSES
- DATA FLOW DIAGRAMS

Templates & Tools
- Business process swim lane map
- Data model
- Data flow diagram
- System reference architecture diagram

Figure 11. The Architecture element of data governance

Architecture can be defined as "the organized arrangement of components to optimize the function, performance, feasibility, and/or aesthetics of an overall structure." (Earley, 2011) In simpler terms, architecture is the highest level of design governance—it guides how we think about our business and provides rules for building business solutions.

We will describe the enterprise data model at the conceptual level, which could be the foundation upon which all data solutions will be built.

The goals of the Architecture element of data governance are to:

1. Define a conceptual data model that meets the business needs.

2. Identify the mandatory or "golden" fields that need to be governed and managed.

3. Document related data flows and business processes.

4. Document reference architecture for data stores.

The Architecture data governance data element covers both business architecture and technology architecture. Types of outputs from working this element are things like business process flow diagrams, data models, data flow diagrams, data category charts, and reference architecture diagrams.

Inputs into the Architecture element could be data roles, responsibilities, decision rights, and high-level business needs for the data defined in #1 Organization. You may already have an action plan put together to deliver some of the Architecture outputs that you could use as input. Any related technology standards, guidelines, or policies may be referenced in this element.

Data model

A **data model** is a structure that represents real-world data objects that are important to the enterprise, their descriptions, and their interrelationships.

A data model provides an inventory of the data elements that comprise the data subject area to be governed. Within this inventory, certain data fields are required for the record to be considered complete. Identifying these critical fields is an important step because these fields will be the primary input for the data governance phases that follow Architecture.

Data models can be built at different levels, from one for the enterprise to one for a specific data store for a specific application. Model data to the degree necessary to understand the data and its relationship to other data to be able to do impact analysis when preparing for system or reporting changes.

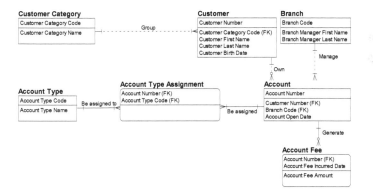

Figure 12. Data model example

Enterprise data model levels

Data domain

A data domain is a defined grouping of related data elements that are completely distinct from other domains. Each domain should eventually have one and only one domain owner responsible for understanding all stakeholder requirements for the data within the domain and developing the domain to meet those requirements.

Data category

A data category is a data subject area containing data of a similar nature that is the highest level of aggregation within our enterprise data model map. A data category may contain multiple data domains.

Data element

A data element is the smallest unit of meaningful data within a data domain.

The State of Tennessee's Data Category Model, also called the Data Domain Model, identifies the top-level Data Categories and their associated Data Domains.

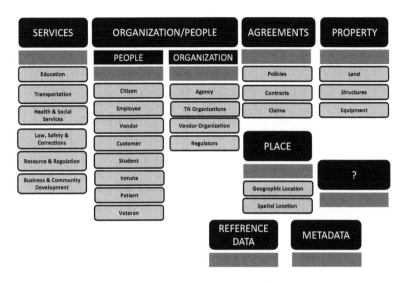

Figure 13. State of Tennessee data categories

Data category

Based on your industry, you will have some similarities with this chart, but you may also have new or different categories as well.

- **Product** – this represents the product lines or products your company sells. This category contains data related to the logical definition or design of a physical object of interest.

- **Service** – this represents the various services your company provides. This category contains data related to the logical definition or design of a service.

- **Organization/Person** – this represents a person or an organization that is part of or interacts with your company. This category identifies the actors and/or performers of actions. It is also many times called a "Party." An Organization/Person is an intelligent entity capable of participating in an event within the enterprise. Organization/Person domains include Organization, Person, and Mechanism/Devices.

- **Agreement** – this represents policies, contracts, or claims. This category is a Rule, Value, or Role defined by a responsible Organization or Person to identify, provide or restrict a specific meaning of a particular data element or enterprise activity. Agreements are used to classify Type or Kind of a Services, Organization, Person, or Event. Agreements refer to information (data domains or data elements) that describe specific business meaning with respect to legal, financial, or regulatory rules that govern how we conduct business.

- **Property** – this represents the assets owned by your company. This category contains the physical properties owned or managed by the enterprise. Property may have multiple relationships to an Organization/Person (Owned By, Managed By, Used By, Controlled By, Stored By, Occupied By, etc.). Property is typically located at a Place.

Property Domains include Assets, Inventory, and Connected Products. Assets include Real Estate, Vehicles and Equipment, Devices, Intellectual Property, etc.

- **Place** – this represents the mappings of areas important to your company. This category defines a physical or logical environment, indefinite region, or expanse. The Place Domains include Geographic Location and Spatial Location. This category identifies a specific state, country, region, government division, population center, etc. A Place may also be an internal view of some Geographic Location(s). Examples of Geographic Locations include County Code, State Code, City Code, Field Area, Census Block Group, Mail Code, Area Code, City State Code, Longitude, Territory Code, and Latitude. Spatial Locations identify a logical or physical portion of a Place. Examples of Spatial Locations include Building Codes, Wing, Floor, Grid, Storage Areas, Lot, Cube, Desk, and Room.

- **Reference Data** – this is common data used company-wide such as "accounting codes." This category defines the set of permissible values to be used by other data fields. Reference data gains in value when it is widely reused and widely referenced. Typically, it does not change very much in terms of definition apart from occasional revisions. Reference data often is defined by standards organizations. Typical examples of reference data are: Units of Measure, County Codes, Corporate Codes, and Fixed Conversion Rates (e.g., weight, temperature, and length).

- **Metadata** – this is data about the data such as owner, data definitions, and the update cycle. Metadata is data or information that provides information about other data. It is a bit confusing by definition but very valuable in practice. Metadata includes data owner, data definitions, data descriptions, technical information about data, etc. It is simply data about the data.

Data flow diagram

As described by Wikipedia.com, "A data flow diagram (DFD) is a graphical representation of the "flow" of data through an information system, modeling its process aspects. A DFD is often used as a preliminary step to create an overview of the system, which can be elaborated on later. DFDs can also be used for the visualization of data processing structured design.

A DFD shows what kind of information will be input to and output from the system, where the data will come from and go to, and where the data will be stored. It does not show information about the timing of the process or information about whether processes will operate in sequence or in parallel which is shown on a flowchart."

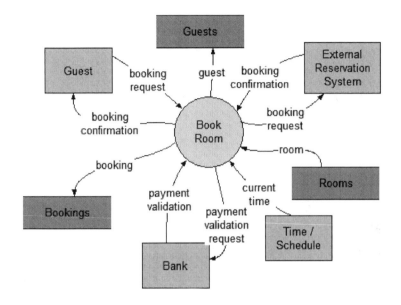

Figure 14. Data flow diagram example – hospitality (Wikipedia: https://bit.ly/3tCukEa)

Business Process Flow Diagram

A business process flow diagram is typically a process flow type of diagram showing the order of events of a business process and the person or group carrying out each step.

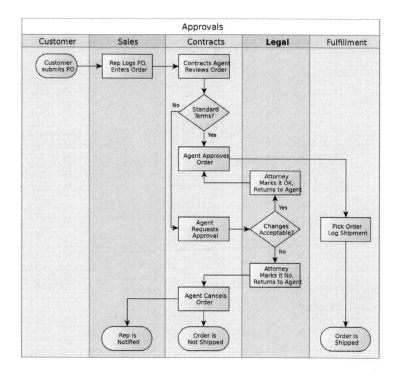

Figure 15. Business process flow diagram example – approvals (Wikimedia https://bit.ly/3tAJwBZ)

Reference architecture diagram

A reference architecture diagram is a diagram of a given technology platform and, in this case, we would be interested in those for which the data going under governance will be traveling through and being stored.

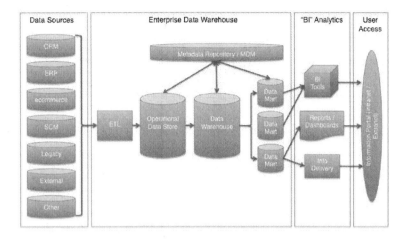

Figure 16. Data warehouse reference architecture diagram (Wikimedia
https://bit.ly/3ntPoMq)

Record layouts and identification of critical data elements

A record layout would be a good piece of information for the Architecture element of data governance. It describes the data contained in the file, the data field name, the data type, and describes how the data is structured or organized in the file.

Customer		
Field Name	Data Type	
Customer Number	AutoNumber	The unique number assigned to each Customer.
Customer First Name	Text	The first name of the Customer.
Customer Last Name	Text	The last name of the Customer.
Customer Birth Date	Date/Time	The date the customer was born.

Figure 17. Record layout example

How to identify critical data elements

Here is a simple yet useful decision tree to aid in identifying critical data elements.

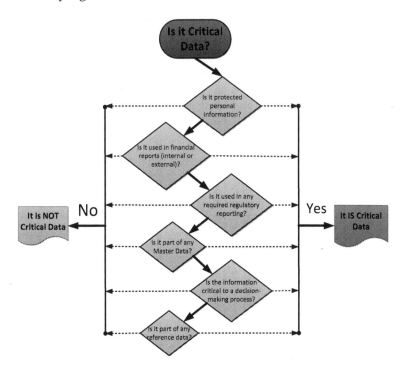

Figure 18. Critical data element decision tree

Architecture playbook

The following are questions to trigger action for the Architecture. In answering these questions and documenting the results, you will be well on your way to completing Element #5.

a. What is the storage location of the conceptual data model?

b. What is the storage location of any physical data models or Data Definition Language (DDL)?

c. Where does this data fit in the Data Category chart?

d. What is the record layout?

e. What are the critical or key fields?

f. Where is the data flow diagram stored?

g. Where are the business processes that use this data stored?

Data administration / controls

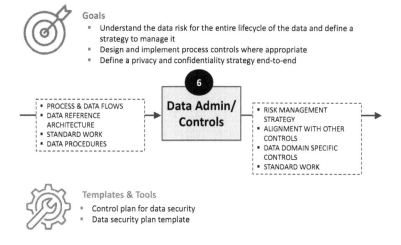

Figure 19. The Data Administration / Controls element of data governance

The Data administration/controls element of data governance is the tie into enterprise data security. The deliverables of this element are related to data access, data masking, data usage, data privacy, backups, and retention. It defines:

- who can and can't have access to what data for what reasons,
- who can create data, how often and where it is backed up,
- how the data should be classified for confidentiality,
- what the retention period is,
- how data is deleted / deactivated,

- when and how the data is encrypted and masked,
- what the disaster recovery plan is for this data,
- what is the end of life, and how the data will be scrubbed to allow for analytic use after its end of life, and
- specifics around any other internal or external control related to the data.

In the data administration / controls element of data governance, the data owner and data steward determine the necessary data governance processes to ensure that the data meets business requirements and enterprise security requirements or policies.

The goals of this phase include:

- Developing a risk management strategy.

- Aligning the data to related controls.

- Developing procedures for managing the lifecycle of the data.

Typically, the data steward will lead this activity with support from the data management team and approval from the data owner.

Inputs into this element of data governance may include the process and data flow diagrams, data reference architecture diagrams, and the data procedures with the documented standard work.

Deliverables from this element may be a risk management strategy, documentation for data domain-specific controls, a reference to alignment with other controls, and the standard work or tasks involved in carrying out the control.

Tools or templates that might prove useful in gathering and documenting data administration and data security controls are a control plan for security and a data security plan template if you already have one at your company.

Administration / controls playbook

The following are questions to trigger action for Data Admin/Controls. In answering these questions and documenting the results, you will be well on your way to completing Element #6.

    a. Who owns the risk management strategy and where is it stored?

    b. Who should have what access to the data and how often is that audited?

    c. Where does the control plan reside and who is monitoring it?

d. What are the applicable data controls?

e. What do internal and external auditors typically look for when they audit?

f. Are there any pending audit findings?

g. Do all of the needed data security policies and procedures exist?

Metrics and reporting

Figure 20. The Metrics and Reporting element of data governance

Performance feedback is an essential component of data quality. The **Metrics and Reporting** element of data governance ensures that defined data quality levels are being regularly monitored so that day-to-day management of the data lifecycle delivers the intended business value. This is not the metrics or reporting that the data is used for, but rather the metrics and reporting done to report on the data quality level of the data being governed.

The goals of this phase of data governance are to:

- Define the "vital few" metrics needed for continuous improvement of data.

- Ensure that the measurement plan aligns with business needs.

- Ensure that the methods for producing metrics are sustainable.

- Establish a reliable and repeatable process for acting on metrics.

The data steward typically leads this work with support from the enterprise data management team and other subject matter experts who can advise the data steward on the existing data quality issues within specific source systems, best practices for measuring various dimensions of data quality, and tools that support data profiling and cleaning.

Inputs to be considered are the data policies, procedures, standards, and established data controls. These artifacts are good indicators of what you should or could be measuring for data quality. The intent is to keep data at a fit for use data quality level.

Deliverables that may come from this element are data quality metrics and processes for monitoring and managing the processes for the metrics. There is no need to measure something if it does not cause action if the measurement falls outside of the control plan. You may also consider giving your data some kind of stamp of data quality certification based on criteria you establish with help from the business or the data governance committee.

Data quality measurements - ATACC

Data quality is the data consumer's perception of whether data is fit for use. Although there are dozens of data quality measurements, this data governance framework has selected five critical data quality dimensions. Depending on the data quality condition of the data domain, more or less metrics may be needed.

- Accuracy
- Timeliness
- Accessibility
- Completeness
- Consistency

Accuracy

Data accuracy refers to whether data correctly reflects the business objects or events they represent. Accuracy may itself be broken into dimensions including:

1. Validity
2. Correctness
3. Uniqueness
4. Format

In most cases, data accuracy metrics should address all the above elements. The specific data quality metric calculation will vary depending on the type of data measured and the business requirements for that data.

Accuracy is the first element in the list because data that is not accurate to begin with will have no value to the end-user. Bad data that is consistent and accessible is still bad data. The table below shows an accurate response to a question and then a violation of each of the five dimensions of accuracy.

Question: *What is the street address of the Tennessee State Capitol?*

Data Value	Condition	Description and Consequence
600 Dr. M.L.K. Jr Blvd	Accurate	Correct value and format.
600 Dr. J.F.K. Blvd	Not Valid	There is no such address in Nashville, TN.
700 Dr. M.L.K. Jr Blvd	Not Correct	700 is not the correct number.
600 Dr. M.K. Jr Blvd	Not Correct	Street name is misspelled.
600 Dr. M.L.K. Jr Blvd 600 Dr. M.L.K. Jr Blvd	Not Unique	Two records match. This is wasted space and can create doubt in the mind of the data consumer.
Dr. M.L.K. Jr Blvd 600	Wrong format	For human consumers, the wrong format can reduce readability and delay comprehension.

Timeliness

Timeliness is the degree to which data is updated at the required interval for a specified business use. The following factors drive the update frequency:

1. The rate at which facts underlying the data naturally change.

2. The speed with which data consumers can act on the data and make a difference.

3. The feasibility and cost of updating the data versus the value of updating.

These three factors must be carefully considered and balanced when setting quality standards for timeliness. So called "real-time" data updates may seem attractive at first, but the business impact should always be the primary guiding principle.

Examples of questions to consider when setting timeliness standards:

- Would frequent updates drive noise into the system?

- More frequent updates may mean greater storage cost. Is the added cost justified?

- Is there an impact on system performance?

Accessibility

The degree to which data is available where and when needed to perform job duties or answer business questions. Accessibility is driven by business needs and is also governed by requirements to ensure that only authorized users have access to data for authorized uses.

Measuring accessibility from a data consumer perspective should focus on:

1. How fast the users can find the data they need.

2. How fast the users can extract the data they need in a usable form.

3. How easy it is to access the data.

Initially, these metrics are probably best measured as sampled values or qualitative indexes, such as a standard usability score for a specific data access method. As data governance and management matures, it may be possible and desirable to set service level agreement values for data availability and load speeds. As with the other dimensions of data quality, the specific metric needed will vary by data set and use case.

Completeness

The extent to which required data has been accurately recorded. Three common situations exist when defining "required" about completeness. The data element is either:

1. Always required or

2. Conditionally required based on the presence or absence of another element

3. Can acceptably be used at a lower data quality level

When defining completeness metrics, specifying the level at which the metric is applied should be included in the definition.

Level	Basic Completeness Definition
Individual Record	Number of accurately populated fields as a percentage of the total fields in the record.
Entire Dataset or Source	Number of complete records as a percentage of the total number of records in the data set.
Enterprise	Number of data sets belonging to a given domain that meet the defined completeness levels as a percentage of the total number of data sets belonging to the data domain.

Consistency

The degree to which data elements across multiple sources correspond with each other on four dimensions:

1. **Meaning**: The definitions and business rules for inclusion in the data set

2. **Naming**: The way the data element is referred to within the data set and by data consumers

3. **Format**: The way that data values are expressed in the system of record

4. **Referential Integrity**: The way the data relates with other data

Example:

Data Source A does not include employees in the definition of "supplier," so no employees show up as records in the data set. Data Source B has no recorded definition of "supplier," but the data set is named "supplier," and includes records for company employees because of the way the business unit processes paychecks.

This difference in meaning between the definition of "supplier" in the two data sources will lead to unreliable answers to business questions related to the number of suppliers.

Consistency is a foundational requirement for integrating common or shared data to provide a "common picture" of information that has enterprise-wide impact. It is also among the most difficult to achieve and maintain in environments with multiple systems which have different underlying data models and business rules. Establishing a strong data stewardship capability is critical to enforcing consistency in such environments.

Certification of data

For some data, certification levels may be established to summarize these dimensions for data consumers and create "trusted sources" for the data curated by enterprise data stewards. The specified quality standards would vary by data domain, but the basic concept for levels of data certification is illustrated in the table below:

Certification	Source and Quality	Quality Level
Verified **Certified**	Source known and data quality measured	Meets defined standards
Verified **Uncertified**	Source known and data quality measured	Does not meet defined standards
Unverified	Source and/or data quality unknown	Unknown

The purpose of data certification is to provide enough information to make an informed decision about the level of risk data consumers assume when using the data. If verified uncertified and/or unverified data is remediated to meet domain standards, it can be reclassified as certified.

The "unverified" designation is quite different. Data of unknown quality or origin may have high information value for providing business insights. Still, the lack of certainty makes such data inappropriate for most normal business purposes such as reporting, dashboards, and triggering of data-dependent operations. Data that is initially classified as unverified can be reclassified into a verified category once research is done to meet defined standards and the data is potentially put under data governance.

In addition to accuracy, timeliness, accessibility, completeness, and consistency for measuring data quality, here are ways to measure the business value of doing data governance.

Measuring business value for data governance

Metric	How to Measure	Business Value
Analyst time finding/ cleaning data vs. analyzing data	Time reporting	Increased Efficiency/ Reduce Time to Business Insight

Metric	How to Measure	Business Value
User Satisfaction with data	Data User Satisfaction Survey	Increased Data Literacy
Number of report requests	Service tickets requested	Increased Efficiency/ Increased Data Literacy/ Reduce Time to Business Insight
Number of people trained in data governance	Learning Management System records	Increased Data Literacy
Time to Complete Data Projects	Project Metrics	Reduce Time to Business Insight
Compliance with Regulations	Compliance/ Audits	Risk Reduction
Number of data issues identified/escalated to Data Governance Committee	Data Governance Committee	Increased Data Literacy
Number of approved and implemented standards, policies, and processes	Data Governance Committee	Risk Reduction
Number of published data definitions	Data Governance Committee	Reduce Time to Business Insight/ Increased Efficiency/ Increased Data Literacy

Metric	How to Measure	Business Value
Number of data fields traceable from source to use	Data Governance Committee	Increased Efficiency/ Increased Data Literacy
Number of duplicate data fields	Data Governance Committee	Increased Efficiency/ Risk Reduction
Percent of data validated at source	Data Governance Committee	Increased Efficiency/ Risk Reduction
Percent completion of data attributes	Data Governance Committee	Increased Efficiency/ Increased Data Literacy
Percent completion of data lineage	Data Governance Committee	Increased Efficiency/ Increased Data Literacy
Shorter or fewer batch cycles	Data Governance Committee	Increased Efficiency

Tools and templates that can be used for the metrics and report data governance element might include the definition of the data quality metric, how it is calculated and control charts to know when metrics being report are out of control. You may already have audit templates and processes that could be leveraged here. You should have a root cause corrective action process so you know who is taking what action if the data quality level falls below the fit for use level.

Metrics and reporting playbook

The following are questions to trigger action for the Data Governance Element #7 of Metrics and Reporting. In answering these questions and documenting the results, you will be well on your way to completing Element #7.

a. What metrics are being tracked?

b. How are the metric(s) being tracked?

c. Who is tracking the metric(s)?

d. Where are the metrics being stored?

e. Who sees the metrics?

f. Who acts on the metrics?

g. What is the process for collecting, managing, and acting on data quality metrics?

h. What actions are taken if the data quality metrics go out of the data quality control levels?

Audits

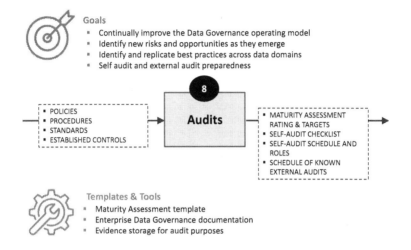

Goals
- Continually improve the Data Governance operating model
- Identify new risks and opportunities as they emerge
- Identify and replicate best practices across data domains
- Self audit and external audit preparedness

8

- POLICIES
- PROCEDURES
- STANDARDS
- ESTABLISHED CONTROLS

Audits

- MATURITY ASSESSMENT RATING & TARGETS
- SELF-AUDIT CHECKLIST
- SELF-AUDIT SCHEDULE AND ROLES
- SCHEDULE OF KNOWN EXTERNAL AUDITS

Templates & Tools
- Maturity Assessment template
- Enterprise Data Governance documentation
- Evidence storage for audit purposes

Figure 21. The Audits element of data governance

The **Audits** element of data governance ensures the data governance process is self-auditable as well as externally auditable. The deliverables and artifacts behind the eight elements of data governance should be documented with links to evidence. If your company is internally or externally audited for data governance or data management practices, everything will be in one place, thus eliminating the mini project that begins when an audit starts. The purpose of the self-audit is to set up a regularly scheduled event to audit that the data governance processes are being used, the data policies are being enforced, and the data quality metrics are under control, impactful, and causing action.

Typically, the data owner determines what needs to be audited and what the self-audit schedule should be. The data owner is responsible for performing the audit and reporting its results. This keeps the data owner in touch with the data and its quality levels on a regular basis.

The goals of this phase include:

- Working through a self-audit process.

- Documenting any gaps in the data governance and developing work plans to close the gaps.

- Reporting of the results of the audit to the data governance committee, leadership, and data consumers.

- Being prepared for internal and external audits.

The inputs should be your data quality policies, procedures, standards, metrics, and controls since this is what the data owner will be auditing to make sure you are doing what you should be doing to govern the data and that the data quality level is remaining at a fit for use level.

The deliverables from this final element may be a data maturity assessment rating and some targets set to improve the data quality level. You may develop or may already have a template for a self-audit checklist to remind you of the steps that need to be taken for a self-audit and to prepare for an external audit. You will most likely create a calendar of when to audit what and when known other audits typically happen. You will want to document the roles and functions that need to be involved in an audit.

Tools and templates to consider for this ongoing function might be a data maturity assessment template or process, a form or template to capture the audit results, a place to store the completed audit document(s), and any related evidence or findings.

Here is an example of a data governance self-audit checklist:

Data governance self-audit checklist

1. Assess the maturity of the data domain.

2. Create a task list to address any gaps in data maturity.

3. Is all data governance information for this data domain stored centrally with links to evidence?

    a. Published policies
    b. Documented procedures
    c. Data standards and definitions
    d. Data flow diagrams
    e. Business process charts
    f. Data controls

4. What classification is your data?

5. If Confidential or Sensitive, what regulation is it? (i.e., PII, HIPAA, CJIS...)

6. What are the people and assigned roles associated with the data, and are they trained?

    a. Data owners
    b. Data stewards
    c. Data custodians
    d. Data consumers
    e. Data producers

7. How does data leave your area of control?

8. What data sharing agreements are in place? Are they still in date or need to be updated?

9. Do you have an updated RACI?

10. What are the data quality metrics and how are you addressing them?

11. What is the self-audit schedule?

12. Are your data quality metrics in control? If not, are there plans underway to correct?

13. Has progress been made to correct known data issues?

14. Are there any known upcoming audits, either internal or external planned that may need preparation?

Assessment and audit playbook

The following are questions to trigger action for Audit. In answering these questions and documenting the results, you will be well on your way to completing Element #8.

a. Do you need to assess the maturity of the data domain?

b. Is all data governance information for this data domain stored centrally with links to evidence?

c. Is there a task list to close gaps in future iterations?

d. What is the self-audit schedule?

e. Do you have a self-audit checklist?

Conclusion

So where do you start? What data deserves data governance the most?

One way is to create a Pugh matrix to prioritize critical or key datasets. Below is a template you could use with

"Concept 1, 2, 3, etc." across the columns being sets of data. The rows consist of Requirements Criteria and/or Constraints pertaining to the sets of data. The Weight column is a place to apply a factor making some criteria or constraints relatively more important than others. '

Data Governance/Data Management Prioritization Matrix																	
	WEIGHT	Concept		Concept		Concept		Concept		Concept		Concept		Concept		Concept	
Requirements Criteria/Constr.		Rating	Weighted Score	Rating	Weighted Score	Rating	Weighted Score	Rating	Weighted Score	Rating	Weighted Score	Rating	Weighted Score	Rating	Weighted Score	Rating	Weighted Score
DQ - Accuracy	1		0		0		0		0		0		0		0		0
DQ - Timeliness	1		0		0		0		0		0		0		0		0
DQ - Accessability	1		0		0		0		0		0		0		0		0
DQ - Completeness	1		0		0		0		0		0		0		0		0
DQ - Consistency	1		0		0		0		0		0		0		0		0
Availability of staff	2		0		0		0		0		0		0		0		0
Impact to business	2		0		0		0		0		0		0		0		0
Difficulty of iteration	2		0		0		0		0		0		0		0		0
Size of iteration	1		0		0		0		0		0		0		0		0
TOTAL			0		0		0		0		0		0		0		0

Scoring Key:

DQ - Accuracy	Existing data provides conflicting answers to the same questions across business departments and between reports and/or systmes. Higher score if
DQ - Timeliness	Existing data is not delivered "on time" or does not contain the correct timefram fo data. Higher score if this is true.
DQ - Accessability	It is difficult to get to the data or data must be manipulated after you get it. Higher score if this is true.
DQ - Completeness	Data has "holes" in it. Missing data. Higher score if this is true.
DQ - Consistency	it's not always possible to compare "apples to apples". Higher score if this is true
Availability of staff	the staff that might resolve this are available to assist. Higher score if this is true
Impact to business	Overall positive impact to on-going business. Higher score if this is true.
Difficulty of iteration	This may be a fairly simple idea to resolve because of the data involved and the low number of departments involved. Higher score if this is true.
Size of iteration	This may be a fairly quick idea to address. Higher score if this is true.

Figure 22. Pugh matrix example

The highest score may help to identify where the most value for the effort will be achieved. Ideally, this is how you would prioritize and determine where to start on your data governance journey.

But from one practitioner to another, it does not always work this way. More often than not, I find myself starting with the "willing"—those who already understand the value of data governance and will be good partners to work with. This is not a bad strategy, and it helps to build credibility in the data governance work you are doing. It provides an example for others to learn from and to replicate. After I have worked on all of the "willing," I then start researching and building tailored use cases for potential candidates. I create benefits calculations and/or risk reduction plans to drive interest and intrigue into the "what if" and the "what's possible" once you have data under data governance.

How long does this take to complete?

Like a lot of things, *it depends*. I should also mention it never ends. Typically, a well-defined and well-scoped set of data can take 6-12 weeks to make your first pass through all eight elements of the data governance framework. At the end of that activity, you will have a work plan of items that need to be done to close the gaps and fully have the data under governance. These work items would need to be prioritized and worked. As time goes by, there may also be the need to update the data governance process or artifacts for the data because of changes to the data, its processing, the data quality level, the roles, etc.

How do you start?

Below is a sample work breakdown structure of what to consider doing for each of the eight elements. You will notice there is a 0 Element which is suggested prework before the clock gets started.

- Draft scope of data to be governed
- Determine leads from governance and business
- Document the intended high-level benefits
- Create a common place to store all artifacts
- Determine communication cadence
- Host a kickoff meeting
- Ensure there is executive support

- Determine team and roles
- Train on the data governance framework
- Draft a RACI chart of team members
- Identify producers of the data
- Identify the consumers of the data
- Develop the data governance committee(s)

- Determine what policies exist
- Agree on what policies are needed
- Identify any related policies
- Identify gaps in any policies
- Train on roles

- Find business procedures that create/consume/protects data
- Develop procedures for policies
- Update RACI with new tasks
- Develop communication plans and training plans for the procedures

- Identify key/critical data elements
- Document any valid values/pick lists
- Document data dictionary/business glossary
- Draw a data model if applicable
- Reference any naming standards that apply
- Document business rules

- Create reference architecture diagram
- Create data flow diagrams
- Document record layouts
- Create business process flow diagrams
- Create application flow maps

- Update RACI
- Identify security and privacy requirements
- Identify data controls
- Build a risk register
- Classify data for confidentiality

- Determine data quality targets/metrics
- Build control plans
- Update RACI
- Draft mitigation plans
- Draft communication plan
- Develop process to capture and report
- Identify maturity assessment and targets to improve data quality

- Build self-audit plan and schedule
- Confirm consolidated evidence recording is occurring
- Update RACI
- Develop external audit schedule
- Build plans to close any gaps

CHAPTER 5

Documenting the Data Governance Playbook Results

Here is a template that can be used to document everything that was completed while working through the eight elements of data governance. It will be used to manage data governance for a defined scope of data. It will capture all the relevant information needed to manage and practice data governance for that defined scope of data. It can also be used at times of self, internal or external audits. As it has been mentioned before, this is your "three-ring binder" that you will use to self-audit and hand to other auditors. New employees can also use it for onboarding or for your IT staff or consultants to better understand the data, its flows, its architecture, ownership, roles, etc. By having this, you have data at a fit for use data quality level (or on its way to be), it has action plans if it falls below the defined level, and in one place you have documentation on everything there is to know about this governed data.

This documentation should be versioned and stored in a central data governance location. It will be owned the by the representative data owner.

This documentation will be created while going through the initial process of putting data under data governance. The data owners and data stewards will update it as governing conditions for the data change over time.

DATA GOVERNANCE DOCUMENT

DATE CREATED		DOCUMENT NAME	
VERSION NO.		CREATED BY	

I. BACKGROUND

What is the key or critical data being covered in this document and why?

II. DOCUMENT PURPOSE

What and who will use this document, how and why?

III. DOCUMENT SCOPE

What this document does and doesn't cover.

IV. BOX 1 – ORGANIZATION

ROLE	RESPONSIBILITY

I. BOX 2 – POLICIES

NAME	LOCATION / LINK

II. BOX 3 – PROCEDURES

NAME	LOCATION / LINK

III. BOX 4 – STANDARDS & DEFINITIONS

TERM	DEFINITION / VALID VALUES / DATA TYPE / GLOSSARY LINK

IV. BOX 5 – ARCHITECTURE

Data flow diagrams, business process flow maps, reference architecture diagrams, data definition language, etc.

V. BOX 6 – ADMIN & CONTROL/SECURITY

A. DATA ACCESS	
B. DATA USAGE	
C. DATA SECURITY	
D. DATA PRIVACY	
E. DATA DESTRUCTION	

I. BOX 7 – METRICS & REPORTING

Description of the data quality metrics and why they were chosen.

METRIC TYPE	METRIC NAME/DESCRIPTION	LOCATION / LINK

II. BOX 8 - AUDITING

How often and who will audit? Link the evidence in the chart below.

MATERIAL TYPE	NAME	LOCATION / LINK

III. CONTACTS

NAME & TITLE	PHONE	EMAIL

References

Bergson, A., and Dubov, L. (2011). *Master Data Management and Data Governance*. New York, NY: McGraw Hill.

Earley, S. (2011). *The DAMA Dictionary of Data Management, 2nd Edition*. Denville, NJ: Technics Publications, LLC.

Ladley, J. (2012). Data Governance: How To Design, Deploy, and Sustain an Effective Data Governance Program. Waltham, MA`: Morgan Kaufmann.

Loshin, D. (2009). *Master Data Management*. Burlington, MA: Morgan Kaufmann.

Mosley, M. (2008). The DAMA-DMBOK Functional Framework.

Mosley, M., Brackett, M. H., and Earley, S. (2010). *The DAMA Guide To Data Management Body Of Knowledge*. Technics Publications, LLC.

Seiner, R. S. (2014). Non-invasive Data Governance: The Path of Least Resistance and Greatest Success. Basking Ridge, NJ: Technics Publications, LLC.

Loshin, D. (2010). The Practitioner's Guide to Data Quality Improvements. Burlington, MA: Morgan Kaufmann.

Index

Made in the USA
Middletown, DE
09 December 2021